The Little
Prop

G000144921

Your property journey
starts here

Chapter 1

Thank You

Such a simple phrase and one that is so often forgotten or underplayed. None of our successes in any aspect of our lives would have been possible without the unfaltering support of our loved ones and our professional Power Team(s). Although challenging at times, we are grateful for every obstacle and every opportunity that has crossed our path over the years.

We thank Sport for allowing us to express our athletic talent. Our journey has been a privilege. From sport to family, business and now property, we truly hope that The Little Book of Property, created in conjunction with our valued friends and colleagues at Perform in Property™, will inspire you to take action and create your own Legacy through bricks and mortar.

Steve Backley & Roger Black

PERFORM in
>>>> PROPERTY.

Why Property?

Both Steve Backley and Roger Black, two of Britain's greatest ever Olympians, changed the world of sport and British history in some way during their professional sporting careers. Such a legacy cannot be fathomed or imagined by most of us, particularly the scope of their achievements at such a young age.

Steve is the first individual GB athlete in history to have medalled at three consecutive Olympic Games from 1992 to 2000. In 1991, Roger and his fellow 4 x 400m team members took a huge gamble that paid off at the World Championships in Tokyo to became world champions. But no success is achieved without taking risks and consistent positive action or developing the occasional feeling of self-doubt.

Some readers might not initially 'get' the direct link between sporting success and property investing. For Steve and Roger, the psychology of winning is both consistent and complementary with success in any guise. Steve and Roger have created a performance model, based on five fundamental key success traits that they have observed in high achievers. Traits that can offer a development model for you as a future property investor.

FIND YOUR
PASSION

CREATE
EMPOWERING
BELIEFS

POWER
THROUGH
CLARITY

SURROUND
YOURSELF
WITH TALENT

DELIVER YOUR
MAXIMUM

© BackleyBlack 2005

6

The fundamental questions you should be asking yourself before starting out are…

1 Have you already found your passion?

Do you really know what and why you are doing what you are doing? If so, do your actions concur with this approach? Does your current lifestyle give you more time and more freedom? If not, property investing can help give you more time and money to choose how you spend your time and with whom. Steve and Roger encourage individuals to take time to establish clear personal and professional values. This is a key starting point in your property investment journey.

2 What do you believe is possible?

Steve and Roger are fully versed with the challenges associated with self-limiting beliefs. What we think, we 'become', and as Olympic athletes, failure isn't a mental option. Those 'little voices' in our head are our worst enemy and hold us back. Whether they derive conditioning from our formative years or whether they are self-imposed, you need to start believing that the very impossible IS possible. Perhaps look at triggers and what you believe is truly possible in your lifetime.

3 Do you have clarity of what it is you are trying to achieve?

Sometimes, we need to be reminded of this, especially in an ever-changing, fast-moving world. Take a fresh look at where you are and where you want to be. Be honest with yourself and whilst this can be tough, taking a fresh look at both where we are and where we are going can help align efforts. But fear not as you don't need to do this alone.

4 Do you have the right people around you?

What might you have overlooked in this regard? Do you have the people with the best skills, knowledge and behaviours to help you reach your dreams? Don't be afraid to part company with the 'red-lighters' in your world if need be (the negative people who might try and bring you down, consciously or sub-consciously).

What does your 'maximum' look like?

5 What actions do you need to take to fulfil this? Striving for the next rung on the ladder is key. Small steps in the direction of your ultimate performance will take you there. What can you do to sharpen your saw, to raise your bar and, even in a tiny way, improve what you do?

Every athlete knows that their professional sporting career is finite due to injury or

illness and may take them out of their comfort zone and sometimes into a lonely and dark place. Young athletes starting out on their journey may not necessarily think about their professional or financial futures or might entrust such matters with external 'experts'. They may be too focused on the 'now', their training and the importance of 'winning'.

More recently, retired professional athletes have started to open up about life after sport and this is where property and the creation of passive income streams come into play. Most athletes won't think about passive income creation until their sporting careers are coming to an end. Using hindsight as a guide, Steve and Roger want to encourage you to think about your future NOW and ask what your life looks like in five or ten years' time.

The most important message for you, the reader, is that professional sports people are vulnerable, just like you. Lives can be broken or destroyed overnight. And regardless of whether you are a sprinter, a lorry driver, an entrepreneur working 24/7 or a retired teacher, each and every one of you reading this book can find your passion and create your own version of 'financial freedom' through property, on your terms.

Steve's Property Story

Steve Backley is best known for his sporting prowess, as the first British track and field competitor to have won individual medals at three different Olympic Games. Today, Steve is still passionate about sport but has also transferred his skills from the track to business life. Together with Roger Black, this dynamic partnership created BackleyBlack, a powerhouse of performance knowledge that has taken these two charismatic British Olympians all over the world. Steve and Roger teach corporates and start-ups alike how optimum performance within sport crosses over into life and business, through mindset, mentorship, hard work and teamwork.

What is lesser known about Steve Backley, however, is that he is a passionate property investor, having purchased his first investment property when he was just 19, based on his father's encouragement and wise words.

❝ I grew up in 'Suburban Bexley', as I call it. My father instilled in me from a young age that 'bricks and mortar' was your safest bet when it came to investing, and his words still ring true today. The first house I bought, I purchased in Chislehurst as an investment property as I had started at Loughborough University and didn't need it as my primary residence, per se. I was 19 years old, the world junior record holder for javelin and thought I knew everything. I didn't but as someone I know always says, 'hindsight is a genius.'

This route to a part-time property investing career was fairly unusual as most people buy their first property as a home and then branch out. It wasn't long before some cracks appeared in my plan. I was completely focused on my athletics career and panicked when interest rates went up. A property that I had paid £107K for, I sold with negative equity, for £97K, when interest rates hit double figures. Had I had the correct training from experts as well as the right mind set and more confidence, I would have kept the property and simply changed my strategy to fit the macro situation. **❞**

Steve sold this first property to a man whom he coincidentally sat next to at a property auction many years later, when both had advanced in their respective property investing careers. Even at that age, Steve instinctively knew that he needed to find a regular passive income to

support his sporting efforts as one day he would stop throwing a javelin. Steve also recommends each and every one of us to consider a secondary, passive income through property investment.

“ Success is a very personal journey and it isn't for me or anyone else to dictate how much money or how many investments we should each have. What works for my mum and dad, for example, isn't necessarily right for me but the principle remains the same. We all have to dig deep to find out what is right for us, where our passions lie and which life path we want to follow. **”**

It took some time for Steve to try again and dip his toe into the property investment pond; it was 10 years later, buying an investment property again in Chislehurst. The reason, he explains, is that he always regretted the mistake of losing confidence first time around 10 years prior. Thereafter, Steve continued to invest, without a set strategy or goal, other than 'Location, Location, Location'. Roll forward to today and Steve has 16 units in his property portfolio based in Sidcup, Chislehurst and Loughborough. This is where the next stage of Steve and Roger's commercial career comes in.

Both parties felt that there was an absolute synergy between successful investing and success in sport and that peak performance in any walk of life is only achievable with the right training, power team and resources.

PERF⃝RM in
»»» PR⃝PERTY.

Perform in Property was launched by Steve and Roger back in 2016, together with Legacy Education Alliance, Inc. (LEA), the world's leading provider of professional and personal development programmes. A new partnership was formed. Since that time, Steve and Roger have been mentored and moved forward as partners in property investment. Within six months, Steve and Roger had sourced and completed five property deals, some as 'baby' property deals for under 100K and others that are slightly more complex. For Steve, this new venture made perfect sense in relation to his property investing career and added:-

❝❝I have met so many students, mentors, trainers and company personnel from LEA and have been blown away by how friendly and supportive everyone is of one another. As someone who is fuelled by competition and winning, I found the company's family-like nature both refreshing and surprising. I would have imagined that a group full of successful property investors might be 'gung ho' and aggressive but this couldn't have been further from the truth.

Some of the real-life stories I have listened to have both moved and inspired me towards the next part of my property investment career. Trainers share their life's work to help others avoid mistakes that they have made in the past. Where was LEA when I sold my first property?

I know that Roger and I have, and will, continue to learn a huge amount from our own training. For me, I am not particularly motivated by money for the sake of money or having lots of status symbols – I have three Olympic medals, after all! I want to retire in my 50's as financially free and have enough money to enjoy the rest of my days, as well as leave a legacy for my children. Without my dad encouraging me to invest in the early days, I might never have found my passion for property later on. I hope I can be as positive a role model to my daughters as my dad has been to me. added Steve, with a smile. **"**

Develop your own 'Olympic' Council

"As an individual athlete my 'team' was less obvious. My team in the run-up to the 2004 Olympic final was 13-strong. I had a 'dream team' of medical, technical, tactical, nutritional and physiological people, all of whom I trusted. Each member of the team knew their role and that of each other's within the team. The quality of that team was ultimately the backbone of my success. It was a different team dynamic to that of a rugby pitch or even a relay, but one that exists in many working environments. As a professional property investor, you rely on your team and the win:win mantra as part of YOUR trusted power team. **"**

Steve Backley

One could say that Roger Black, who was born in Portsmouth in 1966, started running before he even came into this world. Born 32 minutes before his twin sister, Roger was often one pace ahead of the rest. Growing up in a traditional household, Roger attended grammar school, was a good student and aspired to be a doctor, like his dad.

Whilst Roger enjoyed sport as a young lad, he never thought he would build a career out of it. Particularly when he found out, aged just 11, that he had a leaky heart valve, a condition

that has stayed with Roger for life. Sport became increasingly important to Roger over the years. Whilst he never joined a club properly, it was only when he messed up his Maths 'A' Level and took a year off to retake the exam, that he joined an Athletics Club.

The rest, as they so rightly say, is Olympic and Great British History. Roger went on to become the European Junior Champion in 1985, got his grades for Southampton University and pursued a degree in Medicine. After his first term though, Roger realised he wasn't destined to wear a white lab coat and that the white lines of the running track were a'calling.

Roger says of himself that he always gave 100% but wasn't overly competitive. Yet, aged 19, and now as one of Britain's best 400m runners, running became everything. In addition to his heart condition, Roger experienced numerous injuries, but ensured that his mindset was such that he kept going - with the right team around him; positive mental attitude; focus; the best coaches; training partners and a true desire to win.

In 1986, Roger won The Commonwealth Games and European Championships, and with the help of a sponsor, Roger bought his first house, aged 20. Whilst Roger knew he was at the top of his game, he was also more than aware of the fact that injury could stop him running at any point and that his sporting career was finite.

" " Most successful athletes don't get involved in sport for the money. It is usually passion that is the key driver and financial gain is secondary (although welcomed, of course). As a professional sportsman, I was focused, committed to the track and it was only when I was on the outside that I felt more exposed and vulnerable.

Over the years, I often struggled due to injury and had to downsize my property to cover my medical bills. If I had invested in property way back then, I would have a very different portfolio today. Just because you are a good sportsman, woman or business person, that doesn't automatically mean you will achieve success. The formula relies on more than ability alone and this is where I can help others. " "

One of the highlights of Roger's sporting career culminated at the legendary 1991 World Championships' 4 x 400m relay in Tokyo with fellow team-mates Kriss Akabusi, John Regis and Derek Redmond. These spirited GB runners took a gamble by sending Roger out first. They were up against the dominant USA and knew they had to pull out all the stops if they were to win. And win they did, with the best of British teamwork.

" " The mindset for success is similar, regardless of whether you are a 400 metre runner or whether you are launching a start-up or property investing business. As a professional sportsman I know the price I often had to pay for success – the same is true of anyone who wants to reach and stay at the top of their professional game: you make repeated choices and decisions; you focus 100% on the end result and rely on a solid backdrop of team players and mentors to drive you forward. I couldn't have achieved what I have done without having the right people around me.

The ability to change a winning formula is actually a winning formula. I don't believe in change for change's sake; I believe in change for improvement. At the World Championships in 1991 we made a strategic change, not a massive one. We tinkered with the running order. The key was that we made that change around what was, in effect, a very solid foundation. At that moment in time we had four world-class athletes who were ready. That very small change enabled us to go from being excellent to outstanding and champions of the world. Great results start from humble changes, as long as the fundamentals are in place. This belief is as relevant to property investing as it is to sporting success.

Roger Black

Chapter 3

Don't Believe the Hype

The main difference between the professional property investor and his or her amateur counterpart is that the professional will focus on the facts and not listen to 'naysayers' or negative third parties creating panic about the property industry. We can all fall victim to fear-driven media or social media stories about property doom from time to time but the trick is to block out the white noise and to stay focused on our objectives and journey. In reality, for most educated property professionals, they will see an opportunity in adversity rather than doom and gloom, particularly when statistics suggest that more property millionaires are created during a recession than at any other time.

Currently, five million households are in private rented accommodation, a figure that is set to rise to 5.79 million by 2021 (*Source: Knight Frank*). Historically, property prices will double every seven years (outside London) and if understood correctly, the British property industry provides flexibility and opportunities for investors. You, as a next generation professional property investor, have the opportunity to potentially help house a small percentage of the 790,000 people who will be seeking homes over the coming few years (half a per cent equates to 395 households!).

Whilst some of us may wonder how Joe Bloggs in house number four has a new Audi R8 and

is glamming it up with his lifestyle, this isn't necessarily a financial reality. Some homeowners are mortgaged up to the hilt. Having little or no equity in your home or a brand-new sports car does not equate to having a tangible asset or make you 'rich' – the house may 'belong' to the bank and the car may 'belong' to a dealer (harsh but true). A savvy property investor understands the fundamental differences between an asset and a liability and knows the true meaning of 'leverage'. You will learn this on your property investment journey with us.

PERF◯RM in
»»» PR◯PERTY.

Chapter 4

Which Property Investment Strategy to Choose

All of the following involve transferrable skills that YOU can learn. Property investing can take a multitude of guises, both going it alone or working as a cooperative or partnership. For those starting out, here are a few options in terms of the strategies that you might consider. If you want to learn about these strategies and many more, Perform in Property training programmes can help.

Buy-to-Let – What you can learn

- How to find good Buy-to-Let deals
- How to manage the tax implications
- How to find and check that you have a good quality tenant
- How to set up and manage a tenancy
- The safety legislation required to remain legally compliant
- The eviction process and how to serve notice on a tenant
- How to effectively manage maintenance
- How to minimise voids
- Hedging property for the future
- Resources and support for landlords

Checklist

- Understand your credit score
- Buy Below Market Value (BMV)
- Don't listen to naysayers or 'Google' experts
- Ideal for those starting out
- Make sure your figures stack up
- Always allow extra time and budget for delays
- Do your research, location-wise
- Start small and be patient

HMOs - What you can learn

- The Housing Act 2004
- What is HMO?
- Why it might be interpreted differently
- Regulations: HHSRS, fire safety, electrics, gas, signs, accessibility
- Working with Local Housing Authorities (LHAs)
- Different types: Student, bed-sit, flats etc
- Review case studies of HMOs
- Financials, cashflow, what to calculate and how
- Costs of set-up, building, timescales and licence
- Strategies, locations, price points, deposits and research
- Management, operations and systems

Checklist

- Buy Below Market Value (BMV)
- Ideal for those with a little investing experience
- Maximise the use of space if renovating
- Consider target areas with appeal
- Understand the legal requirements
- Be creative and organised
- Great if you are a builder or work with building experts
- Source an on-site manager

Lease Options -

What you can learn

- How to create a Lease Option system that pays you a steady monthly income while you sleep

- How to create contracts that allow you to purchase property for little or 'no money down' and are virtually risk free

- How to spot the opportunity of what makes the perfect Lease Option and how to market and negotiate a 'win-win' offer on a potential Lease Option deal

- A specialist Solicitor will walk you through how to set up legalities and contracts for Lease Options. This will cover what occurs in event of:- Death, Bankruptcy, MIA of all parties

- How to successfully deal with lenders to assume control in the correct way

- A due diligence process to ensure you are protected at all times

- Solid proven strategies to create positive monthly cash flow

- Techniques to help First Time Buyers get their foot on the property ladder

- Techniques to help individuals avert repossession and provide solutions for those that may otherwise struggle

Checklist

- Good for 'buyers' with no deposit

- Find a specialist lawyer

- Ignore rumours – Lease Options are legal

- Bypass estate agents

- Build relationships

- Help those in difficulty

- Think laterally about your portfolio

- Medium to longer term strategy

Social Housing – What you can learn

- Understand opportunities for investors in the Social Housing sector

- Learn to access and employ 'unique tools' available to Social Housing investors such as development grants and other incentives

- Get to grips with relevant legislation, issues and challenges resulting from government-led Welfare Reforms

- Examine Local Authority and Housing Association leases

- Learn about the Local Housing Allowance, Universal Credit and Housing Benefits

- Identify suitable property and locations to target for investment

- Understand how to finance your investments

- Determine how to prepare property to required standards

Checklist

- Supporting local housing stock challenges

- Build local Council relationships

- Up-front, paid-for rent for fixed periods

- Less hands-on if via Local Housing Authority

- If direct, do background checks

- Does this strategy form part of your 'Why'?

- You can't choose tenants if via LHAs

- Consider relevant investment areas

YOUR business checklist

- Understand assets vs liabilities
- Business and financial structure
- Write down a flexible action plan
- Sourcing a trusted Power Team
- Get educated and invest in a mentor
- Do you research
- Consider your WHY
- Include a charitable element to business

The Five P's of Performance
Homage to The Olympics

The Olympic spirit is neither the property of one race nor of one age

Pierre de Coubertin

The Olympic symbol is five interlocking rings on a white background. According to Pierre de Coubertin, the colours of the rings represent the colours that appeared on every national flag from around the world at that time. These five rings represent the five (inhabited) continents of the world: Africa, America, Asia, Europe and Oceania.

For many years the Olympic Games have enthralled generations of people from all over the world. The modern Olympic Games were the dream of Pierre de Coubertin, a French aristocrat, who was motivated to create an event where the vigour and determination of the youth of nations could be an

example of what ordinary people can achieve in an extraordinary environment. However, people who perform at outstanding levels say talent alone is not enough. There are many talented people who never achieve their potential.

Also, a high IQ is not a factor, nor is experience. In fact, many people who have achieved astonishing results have done so in areas in which they had no experience. They were prepared to have the motivation to 'give it a go' and weren't cluttered by limited thinking. The common denominator amongst high-level performers is their drive and courage to seek out advice and absorb ideas from many different sources.

Have you ever gone to a school reunion and wondered why the 'back row' contingent, who were labelled as thick, have somehow surpassed those who appeared to have it all? The real winners develop a set of simple procedures and adopt disciplines which enable them to create an environment of personal excellence. Few outstanding performers describe themselves as being self-motivated from the start. They create this motivation by following rules and disciplines and as soon as self-achievement increases, so does their motivation.

To succeed in any aspect of your life, you need to be at the top of your game, with the right mindset and action plan. Steve and Roger have put together a five-point simple framework to help you at the start of your property investing journey.

Positioning

How to
choose an
investment
strategy
that will
help you
achieve
your life
goals.

*"Take ownership
of your destiny."*

Practice

Investing in
property
is not a
get-rich quick
solution.
Follow a
professional
long-term
system to
generate
sustainable
wealth.

*"Only perfect practice
makes perfect."*

Performance

How a
positive
mindset
and
the desire
to win
are vital
ingredients
for success.

"If you want to continue to be the best in the world, then train and compete like you are the second best in the world."

PERFORM in
>>> PROPERTY.

Problems

How to overcome setbacks and persevere until you achieve your goals.

*"Self-belief is
the foundation
of a great performance."*

Proficiency

Once you've become an established investor, reap the benefits of a passive income for life.

"Success is a decision, not a gift."

The additional 'P' within your property investment journey is 'P' for People.

Your net worth is your network.

You are a direct result of the successes of those around you.

There is no 'I' in team and teamwork is what you need to succeed on your property investing journey.

Property investing checklist

This list is a copy of a press cutting that Steve has kept on his wall for many years as a regular 'note to self'. It introduces 10 statements about actions that you should all consider and implement:-

1. Action is cheaper than planning
2. Action encourages emergence
3. Doing nothing is frightening
4. Motivation follows action
5. Action creates courage
6. We learn from action
7. Action beats the odds
8. Action makes you humble
9. Action overrides fear
10. "Could have", "Should have" and "Would have" - Language we must avoid...

None of you should be left with dismal regrets and thoughts of "What if…". In order not to fall into this trap, you need to be mindful of the language you use and the thoughts you process. The overriding lesson here is to work instinctively and to take action to learn and respond and then act again – create habits. If you don't take action, you are not trying, cannot fail and therefore cannot learn. It all begins with taking action.

The second part of this process is in the appreciation that things might not (and probably won't) happen quickly. Be patient. No-one becomes a surgeon overnight. Olympians don't just 'happen' on a whim or over a few hours on Google. Quality takes time. Patience truly is a virtue. Knowing that success is somewhere down your future path should be a comforting thought.

For Steve and Roger, the single most satisfying aspect of effective property investing is knowing that things are inching towards the intended outcome, whilst life is passing by. How quickly and to what level are two things that may (or may not) be in your control. How aggressively we leverage, often controlled by our perception of risk, will dictate how we position this.

Chapter 6

Mindset

Delivering your maximum

Delivering your maximum is simply about making things happen. Daring to change; daring to step into the unknown; making those tough decisions and acting on them... without delay!

If you have a passion and a belief, then the trait of being able to deliver your maximum will be your Holy Grail. It is about acknowledging there is a space out there, beyond what you currently perceive, to be your maximum and then accessing it. But what does this mean in real terms?

Accessing this space is about having the confidence, courage and commitment to deliver personal excellence. There might be something that is stopping you; if you think it's about someone else, you are already procrastinating. Take responsibility and just make it happen. This can be the hardest or the easiest step to take. It's a choice that we are all obliged to make. Either way, make it happen.

The law of champions

Traditionally, people set goals by using their present state or present situation as a starting point. They look at what they are good at and then try and decide what they need to do to achieve success. Championship thinking does exactly the opposite. Champions dream of the end result and plan backwards.

"See it. Say it. Write it down. The art of setting goals. Champions always write their plans down."

Steve Backley & Roger Black

Think in ink

Winners set themselves up to eliminate any doubt and focus on what they have to do rather than why they might fail. Imagine you are a child, faced with the prospect of a forthcoming exam. The following process focuses on winning actions. Write down what a good result might be for your hypothetical exam. Then create your very own 'success certificate', date it and either get someone to present it to you or have it on your dream board or in your office. This is your goal but you have to write it down and be accountable to you and work backwards.

Begin with the outcome and plan backwards

As per the exam scenario detailed above, start with your defined outcome. Then consider what is required to achieve this goal. In sport, more often than not, you can't guarantee your outcome goal but you can (to a certain degree) define your performance goal. It's the outcome goal that will get you out of bed every morning. This is the dream. This is where the desire and the passion comes from. Your job is to make it 'as likely as possible' that this

will happen. The same concept is as relevant to property investment as it is to taking an exam or competing at The Olympics.

There are three simple principles for you to follow:-

See it: Visualise the end result you want (and be as outrageous as you want!).

Say it: Run it over in your head again and again. Discuss your ambitions with people who can help; get advice.

Write it down: The most important action. Write your strategic plan. Without writing your plan, it will remain a dream and an unfulfilled ambition.

Your focus determines your reality

It is true to say that you get what you focus on. For Steve and Roger, they knew they could and would deliver at the highest level. The fact that their whole lives were devoted to achieving this end – through thought, repetition and written mantra, made it very likely that they could succeed on a consistent basis. Throughout your property investing journey, get in the habit of always envisaging yourself at your very best.

When you talk to champions, one of the reasons that they achieve so much is that they concentrate their focus on what they are trying to achieve in the short term, without ever taking their eye off the long-term goal. They are able to carry both thoughts in their heads, as if on a dual carriageway for success. They realise that the short-term achievement of goals is critical to 'getting going'. It's a step further towards their success.

Go find a buddy

All successful people find like-minded people to work with. If you ask most successful entrepreneurs, or indeed sporting people, they generally come in pairs. They have found someone to start a business with, or they have brought in a trusted ally to help develop a sporting team. Go and find someone who will give you the physical, moral and mental courage to keep you going. Don't be a loner. Forget egos, find more performance friends who park their egos and accept advice and guidance.

Champions are also keen to learn, enquire, listen and understand. The point here is that it's not the ability to store and regurgitate facts, it's in the application of key principles that matters. Delivering supreme performance is not about learning something parrot-fashion; it is about interpreting a situation and then applying knowledge in an effective way.

Experience tells you what to do - Confidence allows you to do it

It wasn't until towards the end of their careers that Steve and Roger realised that there were more aspects of sporting performance that were under their control – more than they had originally thought. The words "I tried my hardest" just didn't cut it later on in their career. A deeper confidence came from the experience of knowing how they had previously reacted in certain situations: eg under pressure or fighting to win when backed into a corner, for example. This became something that they could muster at will. It was something that was instinctive and happened at certain key points throughout their respective careers. They would always look for evidence from previous performances that would give them more confidence to deliver better in the future.

In sport, business, property investing, education or any other performance-related environment, there is substantial evidence to support that the ability to sustain winning thinking, which drives winning performance, differentiates champions from the average. Winning is an 'all-time thing' not a 'one-time thing'. Losers simply can't keep up the mental pace needed. They bottle out for some reason.

P.R.I.D.E

Personal Responsibility in Delivering Excellence

Champions make changes when they are on top of their game - they never get complacent.

It's easy to make changes when things are going badly, when you are injured, when you are getting beaten. At these moments, we often have no choice but to make a big change to survive, and this explains why so many athletes change coaches throughout their careers. The real test is your attitude to change when things are going well and you are on top of your game. In the world of sport there is no room for complacency; if you think you have found a winning formula, then you are about to get beaten. Take P.R.I.D.E in your property investing journey.

"Champions in the world of sport always embrace change. Have the courage to change at the top and you will continue to be successful."

Roger Black

The Sigmoid Curve

'Sigmoid' means resembling the lower case Greek letter, sigma(s). It is a simple way of charting the likely progress of performance for an individual, a group of people or an organization: from start-up to danger of decline. It illustrates that however you reached peak performance isn't necessarily going to keep you either at the top or take you to the next level. You can't keep on doing the same things and expect a different result.

The secret of constant performance is to have the courage to realise when you are at point A and that, despite being at the top of your performance, you need think of ways that you can build on this performance and introduce some changes. In this way, you will start a new

cycle before the first one peters out. The key thing is to remember that the best place to start is at point A – when things are going well.

It is better to keep a top-level performance going than to have to restart and re-energise yourself or an organisation when it is in decline. We all accept change when we have the motivation of success and the energy and resources to do something different. Often, change only comes at point B. The amount of dramatic change necessary is often the death of organisations. They often can't handle what is required, after confidence and self-belief are gone. It is hard for individuals to pick themselves up and move to the next wave when they leave it too late and end up at point B.

Catching the next wave is how champions think. Sport is very competitive. No sooner are you the champion or the market leader than, in every coach's mind and at every company conference, the conversation of those who were out-thought and out-performed is:

"What do we have to do to knock them off their pedestal?"

You have to think beyond number one even to compete the next year; the speeds of copying are immense.

Sigmoid-curve thinking suggests that best practice today is not necessarily the ideal guide to best practice tomorrow; we live in an unpredictable environment.

"Sport doesn't build character,
it reveals it"

We are all a product of our experiences. The past doesn't equate to the future. You may have met people who talk themselves (or you) into defeat with negative comments. They normally start conversations with: "The trouble is..." or people said "The timing's not right for your business" or "The economy will be against you". People who have experienced a 'blast from the past' have felt the impact of others' criticism: "You are no good"; "You will never perform at anything." The thoughts go around in your head, your self-esteem is lowered and you perform poorly. Champions convert these negative thoughts into a determination to prove people wrong. To convert the negative self-talk cycle into the positive.

PERFORM in
>>> PROPERTY.

Chapter 7

Case Study
YOUR Property Story

So Steve and Roger talked the talk, they shared some of their sporting lessons and adapted them into their initial property investing journey, just as you will. Now it was time to walk the walk.

Roger explained, "Steve and I took the next step in our joint investing career. As with any next step, it was scary. Yes, that's right, we felt fearful. Just because we set world records, it doesn't mean we don't get scared, just like anyone else. We do. We just charge at the fear and break through our own self-limiting beliefs."

"Our first joint property investment deal was an HMO (House in Multiple Occupation) in Leeds. After working with our LEA mentor and explaining our short and medium term 'wish-list' strategy, he connected us with some people in the area who might be able to help and form our local Power Team and helped us to structure an action plan.

The first question we needed to ask ourselves was around which strategy we were going to adopt. As we wanted to create cashflow, we opted for an HMO. We bought a three-bedroom house for £87,000 (no, we haven't missed off a 'zero'!), with a view to refurbishing the property into an unlicensed four-bedroom HMO.

We chose Leeds for a number of reasons. Firstly, as it is a growing, diverse city with a range of rental opportunities. We also have contacts in Leeds who could help out if need be 'on the ground'. The property is located near to a train station – a great selling point to increase rentability. The layout of the property leant itself to the proposed conversion and there were no restrictions on planning.

We have been asked why we chose to be mentored by LEA, particularly when Steve already had quite of lot of property investment experience. For us it was a no-brainer. We know, based on our sporting past, that you always learn from the best. And to remain at the top of your game, you need to keep learning. To succeed in any area, you need to leave your ego on one side and look at the bigger picture and listen to others.

For us personally, mentoring matters because it minimises risk. By having the help of a successful property investor by our side, we

better understood the potential pitfalls.

A mentor doesn't offer any sort of financial or investment advice per se, as would a tax advisor or accountant for example. They share with you, lessons they have learnt, more often than not, the hard way. There is a good reason why some of the world's top entrepreneurs will pay many thousands of pounds to be mentored by the best in their respective business field. But all the advice in the world is just advice unless you dip your toe in and take action.

Mentoring allowed us to be slightly more ambitious with the types of deals we considered.

Steve had historically invested in property, looking at the long game and capital growth. Mentorship opened his (and our) eyes to the opportunity of a monthly positive cashflow. The Leeds property, after quite a hefty refurbishment, has actually over-performed. We originally anticipated a £450 rental income from each room per month. The average return on each room in the final event is £480 gross pcm. Win:Win!

So what advice would we give someone who is starting out on their property investment journey ? Just do it! But do it, smart."

Here is a short check-list of priorities, according to Steve and Roger :-

- Invest in yourself and your financial education

- Learn from the best

- Define your 'Why'

- Learn about business structures

- Write down your strategy

- Develop your Power Team

- Operate at a higher frequency

- Steer clear of the 'red-lighters' (negative people)

- Believe in yourself

- Get a property investment mentor

- Make sure the numbers always stack up

- Regularly review your strategy

- Be flexible and have a Plan B

- Learn from mistakes

- Enjoy what you are doing

- Give back and help others

What does YOUR Property Story look like?

Where?

What?

Why?

When?

How?

Who?

What do I want and why?

"What do I want? Be exhaustive, search for masses of content, loads of colour and don't ignore any new thought as you explore all aspects of this – your dream. Spend 10-15 minutes writing. If something comes into your head, write it down and don't stop writing; never let your pen rest. Then, spend the same amount of time again, answering the question: Why do I want it? Again, look for all the relevant reasons. Go back through what you have written and underline everything you think is important and condense it into two statements.

As an athlete, these two statements became the foundation on which to build my plan. Now, as an inspirational mentor to other athletes, I always start with the same question (one that I wish I had been asked time and time again as a young competitor). I always start with: "What is success for you?, and why?" Typically, half of them know what they want (at best) and less than half of them know why. I normally find that the people with the greatest clarity, regarding what and why, are the ones who ultimately achieve. The same goes for you and YOUR Property Story."

Steve Backley

Thank You

Begin YOUR journey and join our TEAM

Thank you for reading The Little Book of Property. We hope this has given you an initial insight into the possibilities ahead of you. Property investing is not for everyone, and like sport or any form of long-term commitment, it requires passion, investment of time and self and sometimes sacrifice. Success doesn't happen overnight and you might not appreciate it as much if it did! Such is the perverse nature of human beings!

We are still on our property investment journey and have now committed to an ever-growing number of deals. We continue to learn and make mistakes (and learn even more). We truly hope that by reading this book you are inspired to take the next step. To take action and attend a forthcoming Perform in Property event. Visit **performinproperty.co.uk** for information on forthcoming events and workshops.

We are really proud of the amazing journey we have travelled to date with Perform in Property and would urge you to become part of our team. Everyone has a gift but sometimes we don't see it or wait until we believe it is too late to showcase it.

Don't be that person who looks back and says "I wish I had…". You are worth more than that.

We believe in you, and so should you. This might be the end of our book but it is just the beginning of your Perform in Property team journey with us.

Steve Backley

Steve was one of Britain's most consistent and popular athletes for over a decade and established himself as one of the all-time greats of his sport having been ranked in the world's top 10 in the javelin every year between 1989 and 2002.

A constant member of the British athletics team, standing on podiums and setting world records, Steve was the first individual British

track and field competitor to win medals at three different Olympic Games: Barcelona, Atlanta and Sydney. Throughout his career, he also became the world's number one javelin thrower, having broken the World Record three times. Steve was also crowned 'World Athlete of the Year' by the IAAF in 1990 and was awarded an OBE in 2003.

Olympic Games

Silver medal	1996	Atlanta	Javelin
Silver medal	2000	Sydney	Javelin
Bronze medal	1992	Barcelona	Javelin

World Championships

Silver medal	1995	Gothenburg	Javelin
Silver medal	1997	Athens	Javelin

European Championships

Gold medal	1990	Split	Javelin
Gold medal	1994	Helsinki	Javelin
Gold medal	1998	Budapest	Javelin
Gold medal	2002	Munich	Javelin

Universiade

Gold medal	1989	Duisburg	Javelin
Gold medal	1991	Sheffield	Javelin

Commonwealth Games

Gold medal	1990	Auckland	Javelin
Gold medal	1994	Victoria	Javelin
Gold medal	2002	Manchester	Javelin
Silver medal	1998	Kuala Lumpur	Javelin

Roger Black

Roger Black is one of the country's most successful sportsmen, having represented Great Britain for 14 years at the highest level in the world of athletics. He is particularly admired for his triumphs over adversity, overcoming serious injuries and a rare heart valve condition, to go on to become a world champion.

Roger won 15 major Championship Medals including European, Commonwealth and World Championship Gold Medals. His greatest achievements were winning the Olympic 400 metre Silver Medal in 1996 and being part of the Gold Medal winning 4 x 400 metre relay team at the 1991 World Championships.
He was British Men's Team Captain and was awarded an MBE in 1992.

Olympic Games

Silver medal	1996	Atlanta	400 m
Silver medal	1996	Atlanta	4x400 m relay
Bronze medal	1992	Barcelona	4x400 m relay

World Championships

Gold medal	1991	Tokyo	4x400 m relay
Gold medal	1997	Athens	4x400 m relay
Silver medal	1987	Rome	4x400 m relay
Silver medal	1991	Tokyo	400 m

European Championships

Gold medal	1986	Stuttgart	400 m
Gold medal	1986	Stuttgart	4x400 m relay
Gold medal	1990	Split	400 m
Gold medal	1990	Split	4x400 m relay
Gold medal	1994	Helsinki	4x400 m relay
Silver medal	1994	Helsinki	400 m

Commonwealth Games

Gold medal	1986	Edinburgh	400m
Gold medal	1986	Edinburgh	4x400m relay

PERFORM in >>>> PROPERTY.

BY **STEVE BACKLEY** AND **ROGER BLACK**

Make-A-Wish grants magical wishes to children fighting life-threatening conditions. Whether a wish is to be a princess or a policeman for a day, meet a favourite celebrity, or just enjoy some special time away from home with their family, a wish come true provides memories that last a lifetime. There are over 20,000 children living with a life-threatening condition in the UK and we would like to help every one of them. All of the money from the sale of these e-books will be donated to Make-A-Wish Foundation® Registered Charity Nos. (England and Wales) 295672 / (Scotland) SC037479. Thank you for your generous support.